#CancelCult

by

Big Sal

#CancelCult

ISBN - 978-1-7347162-5-2

Cover: Jacob "Big Sal" Luna-Cantor
Production: Jacob "Big Sal" Luna-Cantor
Copyediting: Jacob "Big Sal" Luna-Cantor
Research: Jacob "Big Sal" Luna-Cantor

"To anyone who has ever tried to silence what I am expressing by citing my profanity, bad language, or words as justification for this – this one is for your bitch ass."

- Your Daddy, Big Sal

Table of Contents

[Intro]

People cry every day about what constitutes as 'Cancel Culture'.

Women, children, and men are killed daily for failure to conform.

If you abhor the avoidance of injustice

more than actual

injustice,

then you may just be a bootlicker!

(Not maybe actually, but in reality, are)

The Misrepresentation of True Events and the Representation of Fictional Accounts do not often intersect.

I've been falsely accused of many things in my life as well, however what separates this insidiousness from equating me living in fear is the fact that false accusations do not scare me — they define me.

The fact that so many people let falsehoods ruin their lives is the real bitch move.

Sexual predators being held accountable is NOT 'Cancel Culture'.

Believing survivors and victims is NOT 'Cancel Culture'.

The CIA perfected propaganda, but you let it define you.

If I were you, I'd worry a little less about what clothes people wear, what pronouns they prefer to go by, or by what they choose to do with their time than to let it consume me so effectively.

Injustice anywhere is a threat to justice everywhere, yes, and I guess it's also true what they say — one man's trash really is another one's treasure.

Dip & Dab

I curse the blade and sculpture as the nascent fly off handles,

The first to hate a culture is the last to cry it's cancelled,

Our belly crept with age up to still piss down steps at school,

R. Kelly kept the bag up while Chris Brown kept the jewel,

Three to four to pick a fight with respect to split the stone,

We support the shit we like and accept the shit we don't,

Stay born of barren mansions in a fly-by of the terra,

They warned of Marilyn Manson in the hindsight of an era,

Grease no wheel so crushed here softly and stay back to sink this in,

People still show love to Cosby and they'd have a drink with him,

Pluck the rightwing like a Whopper as they pick the parts to press,

Fucking Weinstein in a walker like he didn't force the sex,

To empathize with sick sons if every truth does not crack,

To amp the thighs of victims like Terry Crews had fought back,

Slip this slab into prosecco where we pour 'em in opinion,

Dip and dab unto the deco with decorum in dominion,

Cook the shit in contest with the real sucky people,

Look at it in context and it's still fucking evil,

Crush the beetle in a bind and build new dens to disperse,

'Cause the people of their time were still humans of this Earth.

Ty Cobb

Spit a subtle fleck to us as I hold my facial pad,

Hit the double decker bus like a multiracial ad,

Bitch rules are enabled when you go to rape a soldier,

Minstrels were a staple to appropriate a culture,

Teaching when we shoot it's only now to maybe press the stones,

Even Betty Boop was stolen out from Baby Esther Jones,

A whitened cup of whim as they pick the wall it ruins,

They lightened up her skin and they did it all with nuance,

Shake the team so fall back by the reign that rivers soak in,

Make the screen go all black like your name was Mr. Boseman,

Lift the loudness if as loveless as if you called 'em mixed,

This allowance of injustice is the new politics,

End the sinful town ploys in the seeded vales as aimless,

When the little brown boys can then see themselves as famous,

Find your doubt and rhyme god with a gun to take the decker,

Strike 'em out like Ty Cobb as I run to break the record,

I do facts as pleas suffer on the same small journeys,

Tie two bats to each other like the Baseball Furies,

Cast the basalt birdies as with Kane's bops perching in a bucket of meal,

As I face all juries with the chainsaws dirty in the blood that I spill.

Double-Edged Sword

Gas the campers in the country on the lonely range in labor,

As you pander for the money and the only change is paper,

Truss this dragon with a weapon as the birds near our view,

Just imagine for a second that your worst fears were true,

Grasp the get-up when it sees me and I toss the ball to brother,

As they set up on the TV and they profit while you suffer,

Seek no light if missing out like the blind that stand and break in,

People like to dish it out but they find they cannot take it,

Plus, we're honestly at peace sitting aimed in at the water,

'Cause hypocrisy's disease-ridden blanket is a goner,

Once as tragic as a lich lost *Monopoly* to few,

Just imagine that they're rich off a mockery of you,

Write the truth to mix with dreams and a pelican to perch,

Like to use your pics for memes and then sell it on their shirts,

Court a sore loss and winner at no show to feel the spark,

Or the pornbots from Twitter that'll go and steal the art,

Miss the harpoons if whetted in the flow to still be fed,

If the dark humors get it, then you know you're really dead,

Care to spin dimes and clocks if your heart is missing by no prison?

There's a thin line to walk on this narcissism/nihilism.

George Jacobs

Stay to battle half a prick seeming brave to end the men,

They can cancel Kaepernick, GTA, and Eminem,

Cinch and grip as passion prints prose to toss if at an oak ridge,

Censorship of activists goes across this as unnoticed,

Throw the ball built with breath and the shitty truths to streak,

Logan Paul filmed a death and that Blippi dude's a freak,

Could you punch the two shooters with the nets stuck next to rig?

Put your trust in YouTubers while they mess up *Peppa Pig*,

Bo Jacks is running as he kicks past a stan who he sees high and mighty,

Blow stacks of money as the shit hits the fan like with T.I. and Tiny,

Mute the words that rhyme with 'liar' and the crane goods to take,

Who prefers to find the miner like it's James Woods and Drake?

A pinch to stand inches from the biggest gorge break-ups,

They lynched my ancestors like they did to George Jacobs,

Once the gutter's snow is used, then the day is drinking mothers,

But to suffer's no excuse for the way we're treating others,

Rhyme with the best rhymers to flush the flows once,

Kindness begets kindness in love that grows love,

Stay drunk but then curdled down the payment of sick shit,

They fucked up the world, now we pay them to fix it!

Backyard UFC

You fight with cats and lights when it pays to piss 'em off,

You hype up spats and fights on the day that bets are off,

To book by natural settings when you buy it back to bluff,

You look like rappers wrestling when you try to act as tough,

Growing bones as grass now sits and the black art isn't mercy,

Throwing stones at glass houses when your backyard is as dirty,

I take down increments sold like candlelight of course,

I hate how hypocrites hold to standards high as yours,

Shitting shells to shoot the pharaoh if it helps to teach him PE,

Spinning spells to spook a sparrow on the spelt that speaks as easy,

Skin a mouth that threw its spare nose to a ground that feeds the needy,

Grin at grouse that grew as air grows to the grout that greets the greedy,

Miss the same wall while drinking if the porter is as fatal,

It's an 8-ball we're sinking in the corner of the table,

Go when broken through the backs in the towns that find no free men,

So, we smoke up truth and facts like a lounge that I will lean in,

Go like Gotti at my rivals with my capo capping eyeballs,

So, I body battle finals with a bottle stacking rifles,

Dine with finer men and find a pen to course the switch station,

I'm like Heineken to rhyme again and pour this rich nation.

9.

Fritz ter Meer

Finally carve the totem's tongue if angered as I pass this town,

IG Farben's smoking gun is chambered in a gaseous round,

And Chapo paid his swordsmen for a different wing to cage his,

Monsanto made a fortune by distributing their agents,

Simple as the blame before by this picture of Hell's turrets,

Crippled in the name of war while disfigured and malnourished,

Stack a rhyme and write content as this image burns the fastest,

At a time of ripe conflict is when business turns to fascists,

See a certain cherry climb it if you stake it with a spoon,

We are mercenary-minded if we make it to the moon,

Pass the time so rich with songs and crawl back into corruption,

As we climb Olympus Mons while volcanic in eruption,

Seemingly then spy scents that seas then seize in stone,

Screaming to the sky since the season sleeps alone,

See no semper and a fi if they're pissed at me to piss their wealth,

Please don't enter in to die with a syzygy to scissor self,

Psyche then laid the roads with the prayer played to masses,

IBM made the codes and then Bayer made the gases,

Sumos battle for their places when they feel their lunch was equal,

You don't cancel corporations when they kill a bunch of people.

Rite to Monetize

Pour paint with soda far worse than the kids lost to the frugal,

You're angry over *Star Wars* and you're pissed off like a poodle,

Cut the gauze up in the shower like a dragon in a keep,

Put your paws up on the counter as you beg them for a treat,

They still go through cuts alone if to authorize the song yet,

They will throw you but a bone as they monetize your content,

States that soldier home if there's too few dads a phantom,

Stakes are overdone like they're YouTube ads in tandem,

Abusers are melodic as their song sped to kill me,

The user is the product if the content is still free,

All the gators seeing ducks now that the lake plume is an image,

Small creators being pushed out as they make room for a business,

Best to buy us principle and cut a tad of marlin,

Gentrify what's digital and put an ad like Harlem,

Break your glass with big rocks as I smile afterwards,

Shake your ass on TikTok for the child traffickers,

Push a lie to doubt what's gambled on the whetting of the steel,

'Cause to cry about what's cancelled is forgetting what is real,

Pay us to see the fauns if the fauns hunt the men,

They'd love to free Assange, but he wants Trump to win.

11.

Joe McCarthy

Stay and waggle half as stiff as the cracked cameras do,

They can cancel activists and the Black Panthers too,

I press three blunts into paper if there's hardly cash back,

I guess free lunch is a danger to the starving fat cats,

Mark a Trumpster's foolish feud with his evil guns and country,

Guarding dumpsters full of food from the people just as hungry,

Go unfreeze the door to wreak a war on a corporal's left cheek,

No one needs it more to feed the poor like Immortal Technique,

To take through what is game two to the same few with their laws,

They hate you if they ain't you and they aim through with a cause,

I broke a wrist with slack trust and yolked a bitch if that's fucked,

I almost missed the trash truck where cocoa bits are smashed up,

Kiss mechanical commanders on the farms of weed and grapes,

With a radical agenda and the arms to keep it safe,

Die to storm through in a freedom if the ash has spilled on stones,

I implore you to besiege them in the bastions built of bones,

I can meet you in the forum as the haggis fills the poems,

I beseech you to implore him with the baggage still in homes,

The mass will carry cleaner as the nunneries evolved,

The grass is rarely greener with the companies involved.

12.

Mull a Moment

Dead as most with the handprints that match every tide or pod,

Let us toast to the remnants that have ever died abroad,

Standing kind of by the corpse and in otter lieu of flesh,

And we dynamite the gorge just to honor you in death,

Clear the coast of the crumbs and the cheddar laid in clout,

Here's a toast to the ones that have never made it out,

If a gun busts to scare us, then just know we'll test a bomb,

It's a funhouse of mirrors with the only exit gone,

Find a blade that cuts the gun as it's burning down the sights,

I'm afraid of what's to come when I'm turning out the lights,

Pair this steel disc with flesh if it bites like a mouth,

There's a real risk of death when you fight with yourself,

Store this gun in your ass as I blast it at the laws,

Pour the rum in a glass as I pass it with a pause,

Faced with truth that is filled like the chamomile in brew,

Lace the boots with the silk of this caterpillar goo,

As we catch the killer crew when they punch it through the town,

And we cap the tiller too when he runs it through the ground,

I sealed this writ only by a mountain or the brooks,

I build my crypt slowly while surrounded by my books.

Pol Pot

Lift the nettle tea where beauty is and never be the grooviest,

It's inevitably as dubious if readily we're doing this,

Deck the centuries in misery with porter to sell you lay-offs,

Equanimity's epitome in order to value chaos,

Cut this god's open hell like the livers it'll lend us,

Put the soft-spoken spell on the rivers we'll replenish,

Keep the keys in the club as you sell her like a manga,

Feed the trees with the blood of the pellar with a panga,

Too embossed to set aside if you'll build past the borders,

You can cause a genocide and you'll still have supporters,

Yuck with Ben Stiller's parents if it's fun to holler fast,

Putting ten-dollar garums in a hundred-dollar glass,

Lively apes are in the barrow sipping Karo to drink grapes in,

Ideation of an arrow isn't narrow as creation,

Replace prose with Elvis on the ten toes you owned,

We praise those that help us and condemn those that don't,

We shape this titty business like the cum you thought was paint,

Remake this sticky image to the one you want to hang,

Go nuts and battle vultures for the kill hacked and cut,

So much for cancel culture when they still back you up.

Little Flag Bangs

I throw it down like dumbbells and beat the fucking cop out,

I sow the ground with gun shells and leave it up to God now,

Kiss the chilly sink just barely like a filthy bong and high,

Bitch, you really think you scare me when I really want to die?

Dread the dealings in the city to still hunt rats in the streets,

Better kill me when you hit me or I'll come back for your teeth,

Time to face the Folgers if the pan tastes of grime,

Mama raised a soldier but this man makes it rhyme,

Grip the ice like your bullets as it flips the dead's hearse,

Live your life to the fullest and then give respect first,

Come play and beat this whole hand while still bringing you a bond,

One day I'll be an old man and I'll sing to you this song,

We hit up its girl once its girl meant to suck nuts,

We said fuck the world 'cause the world went and fucked us!

I've missed you in my dreams as I kissed more in the wild,

I'll lift you like the wings that you wished for as a child,

What's a dream to the tome filled with bundles if as moist?

'Cause I'll scream at the stone 'til it crumbles from my voice!

Sold for fun when we're dead as this simple bag hangs,

Hold this gun to my head as its little flag bangs.

15.

Mother Theresa

Pray this burning finger cooks with a cop killer's doobie,

Pay this cursing singer looks like a Todd Phillips movie,

Bubble butts and hands of friends as the ass is fly as parrots,

Couple cups and grams of chems that they classify as careless,

New debris covered FEMA to kill bills blind for laws,

You can be Mother Theresa and they'll still find your flaws,

Bring the hearse into the lead, shot for some to blink and bond,

Be the person that you need, not the one you think they want!

Cedar steeples and a store to throw stone and board the glassless,

Feed your people and the poor, but don't go and court a fascist,

To stand it up in center mass with beats to blitz and blast it,

A planet plucked of Pendergrass as Esham spits his acid,

It pays to lift no shallow firs from deep in town for wood,

They raised their pistol calibers to keep us down for good,

Shambling by bits of smoke here to know peace from afar,

Family Guy did that joke where she ODs in their car,

Like I'm Marshall and a goat if I know it's too much truth,

I'm impartial to a joke but I notice nuanced noobs,

Bust a rhyme that's through a battle with the big dudes in the back,

'Cause to cry that you are cancelled is a bitch move and a half.

Lilyhammer

Go in pairs to the sandal bar if now hating *Gumby*,

No one cares when they cancel art without making money,

To speak in its own broach is to bury ash next to smoke,

Unique in its approach to the very last episode,

Rush away and drive by with a piece to bam-bam!

'Cause I play the wise guy like I'm Steven van Zandt,

A Cutlass to hide Zales like a broke friend as it bets 'em,

I publish despite sales on the low end of the spectrum,

Final fight with ticket times still to battle free for something,

I will write my wicked rhymes 'til they cancel me for cussing,

My stone breaks guns like geysers if the bones and lye are sealed,

I don't make fun of survivors or the homes they try to build,

Try and run if fencing ego like a bottle that won't pitch in,

I am done convincing people when they model but don't listen,

I preserve my grief in rhyme with a yew for bow and cord,

I reserve my peace of mind for the few that show support,

To back into the danger and then dye this deer's stool,

They tap into your anger and then try to appear cool,

Hype the risk to fight 'em off with a friend to strike like clocks,

I persist despite the odds to suspend the spite and plots.

Dr. Seuss

Cooking by this oven when you scoot to fan the flames,

Looking like McLovin when you're super bad with names,

Too hot to play the pundit if stranger to the core facts,

You thought I'd say some dumb shit like anger at the Lorax,

The crux that's in a tomb in confluence of the sea,

The books that you consume will influence and agree,

Who won't cry to burden our book once you write it on the sides?

You don't buy a certain product 'cause you like it or it's nice -

Renew it now in light if it's hard to miss the crypts,

You do it out of spite like a narcissist with kids,

Teach of evil and the prophets as the sons to kill for peace,

These are people in an office and the ones that fill your teeth,

Their guns are at your neck and a hunched back the same,

The ones that cash your check and the ones can't complain,

Stand to burden us with new shit, not cinnamon rolls and tea!

Man, conservatives are stupid, watch the liberals agree!

Add the minerals to soup sips and the herbs are since as free,

And the liberals are stupid as conservatives agree,

Absent, lonely minds still never find the tea to a T,

That's the only time I'll ever rhyme agree and 'agree'.

Emulation of an Exodus

Learn their God's white as a trend if the things you love are right,

Burn the spotlight of a friend if it keeps you up at night,

Send you in the pocket by the buffer to defend the rest to feds,

Then you can profit while they suffer and pretend you never left,

Fear the wicked winds that may come on the same turn of the pass,

Parasitic since on day one like a tapeworm up the ass,

Two to simulate the death of us and still parlay for peace,

You can emulate the exodus but still fall prey to beasts,

Death will free you from the boa if the stipulation bets this,

Etch an emu and a moa if this simulation lets us,

Nearly ride and write five dreams as I tend to sell their fame,

Here we hide the high hijinks like a Penn and Teller game,

To hate the ill and sacred is a vacant cup ignored,

You fake it 'til you make it and then shake it up some more,

Drag the terriers to field as we bury us a shield,

Break the barriers we build like the carriers are killed,

Emulation of an exodus is deathless as a boon,

Trepidation of the best of us has left us in a tomb,

Test the mesh that's in the beans at least if most are faced with stencil,

Press the precious pens appeased to teach of prose replaced by pencil.

Frida Kahlo

Still aim through at the message and a storm in the brew,

They'll paint you as a menace and a thorn in their shoe,

Treat their tar pits like they're trauma as we win a cake at last,

Be the artist that you wanna if you're finna break the bats,

Mostly find kids on the prowl if they play this at their best,

Close these eyelids of an owl if they're anxious and depressed,

Risen rain will eat what's hallowed on the cake by a blessed devil,

Live in pain like Frida Kahlo when you take to the next level,

Which is weaker than a tyrant if we're sick of when we hurt?

Living deeper than a diamond that they dig up from the dirt,

Tip my two new breaths to bless kids that do do best to fetch,

Jip the juju's dress in jest ripped from cuckoo nests in death,

Risk the rubric that I'm making so clowns will halve the folder,

It's as stupid as if saying pronouns are cancel culture,

Alchemists may be history, but folly is the truth!

Now you fist Lady Liberty with Hawley and with Cruz,

Throw the duck a whole piece if to crack it like a window,

So, it's fuck the police and then slap them with the dildo!

To court the same sense as a man dies for pride,

Support your gay friends when they stand by your side.

20.

Social Apes

Beat the stick and play ball on the street to go pop,

Free to shit and say 'bah' like a sheep that won't stop,

A thigh in silk or ribbon thing to eat this pot and burn a sack,

A cry for help so sickening that even God has turned her back,

Pour buckets near a mezzanine that most the graves are vacant on,

For what is there that's left to gain if social apes will make a bomb?

Bloody me with dune winds if it's breezier to find,

Studying the humans is as easy if you're blind,

The shield is cut in two and instilled then in the vision,

We build us up a zoo and we fill it like a prison,

Pick up the station I'd run, sick with the basin's sights gone,

Civilization – Type I – split up the nation – pipe bomb!

Rock the boats when in the sand as a kestrel hunts for two,

Stop encroaching on the land or this death will come for you,

Too pained to purchase scripture with a rock to pack tobacco,

You paint a perfect picture but forgot to add the shadow,

Cards amiss by the drought at the streams I defend,

Narcissists cry for help as a means to an end,

Still learning known looks as they copy us with tiny sumac hairs,

I'll burn my own books on your body just to prove I do not care.

Charles Manson

The crowd now garbled action with a tec to load in case we smoke,

They shout out Charles Manson in that episode of *Raising Hope*,

Weekend thrillers dead as Bowers if more know it's new to rhyme,

Even killers get their flowers before poets do in time,

Supposedly a vision like you fuck the drunk guys now,

Propose to thee in prison while you pluck their punk eyes out,

Drop civility if dreaming that they bust nuts in a sheet,

Probability is pinging as it pushed us to the peak,

I'll dive through like a comet where the jumping bean is skipping,

I'll write you but a sonnet with my bloody fingers dripping,

Spread the dream to see no pulpit if you're dutiful at first,

Rep a scene like Geno Cultshit that's so beautiful it's cursed,

The signs still lead to jumps on the sixth search's term,

My rhymes will eat your lungs like it's Big Lurch with sherm,

Bite no hand to cut me up with as to drill it and then stab,

Syko Sam and Bloody Ruckus as they kill it in collab,

Shoot this puck that bought a pill clutched to flow for real and hours,

Who the fuck I gotta kill just to go and steal their flowers?

I don't know much to war report when I'm par 4 nearer this,

I'm shown more love from horrorcore than hardcore lyricists.

There's That Selective Altruism

Sip like Rambo bought us beer with the cost and flight rising,

Shit, if Van Gogh lost an ear and he tossed at night crying —

Why won't nuts amend the image of no men that sought to brag?

I don't much defend their riches like, "Oh yeah, he got his bag!",

Share the bung covers once we hear the numb nuts while fumbling,

There are young mothers struggling near the dumb stunts of something,

Rethink a book of rhyme as I hope to write this still,

We drink like Crooked I and we smoke like Cypress Hill,

The barren, burning heights crushed to cake where death's sweet,

A parent working nights just to make their ends meet,

So slack and last to drool by the hot smoke on the engine,

Go back and pass the school like a vato on a mission,

Mysteries are gone with ego and the peace to pawn or preach,

It's the cheese upon a Cheeto when your grief is gone at least,

Shoot your ammo at a thousand where nine odysseys are spun,

Move the shadow of a mountain like Diogenes had done,

No new book bleeds in its covers if inspecting something slack,

Go do good deeds for the others while expecting nothing back,

Plus, the rest is all you've risen from a destiny as ample,

'Cause selective altruism is effectively to cancel.

J. Edgar Hoover

Spy the transformation of respect through very dead dust,

Cry for cancellation but forget who Gary Webb was,

Burn us every day in rain with a hollow tip to bless,

Ernest Hemingway complained that they followed him to death,

Feel the hot one like the Devil if he's cooking as he drinks 'em,

Pull the shotgun from his temple as I put it to their kingdom,

Psychos steer while driving east when we store the pain and gun,

I don't fear a dying beast any more than rain or sun,

Dye this latch that locks if I'm down to pull this nightly,

I mismatch my socks and I count my bullets wisely,

Shooters will not catch us if we cover them in pig shit,

Hoover was a fascist with the government complicit,

Stab old pimples in their salience as police will call them guns,

Cancel info on the aliens and release it all at once,

Tinsel town wins the beers of the newly dead for days,

Cancel brown skin for years with the student debt that stays,

Suck the blood of boom bap to still flush men from their blouse,

'Cause I'll cut your bootstraps and I'll stuff them in your mouth,

Temples greet new gods and stuff as they face the kid and cannon,

Then we'll see who's talking tough when you taste the shit you ran in.

$7.50 an Hour of Life

Five cadavers hide the ladder from the men if on the gate,

I would rather buy a dabber than pretend I can escape,

Equal shores adjourn with fears if they're really in pairs and acreage,

People more concerned with peers than the billionaires that rape us,

Tip your bucket greens upon us with the water on the polo,

With more puppet strings than promise like a Robert Johnson solo,

End the equal lies agreed like if Big Boss packed a blade,

When they legalized the weed, I was pissed off at the State,

Tie this brick lost to the regal with the bigger lies to test us,

I was pissed off at the people that had stigmatized my stresses,

Tuck the guns and pad the pyres, seeing some distorting image,

But I wasn't mad at buyers – even Trump-supporting bitches!

I crept by mansions stained dye with a big cup of the lie,

I kept my cannons aimed high at the ship up in the sky,

Stand so new you bet it's never in their face if spinning up rage,

Cancel student debt forever and then raise the minimum wage!

Who's someone so nice in knowledge that they share it with a few less?

Google your price of college and compare it to the US,

Pay a boy his final paper and in lieu of filthy wood,

They'd exploit your child's labor if they knew they really could.

Mao Zedong

Stuck to see more than a slum in a rotten storm as hopeless,

Cut the tree fort to a stump as you swat a swarm of locusts,

So, civilians burden ill men turned to fill ya in and learn,

No vermillion vermin million earned a billion from the burn,

Parse the miso and the lamb if starch is weeks into the pan,

Starving people is the plan when marching eastward in the land,

Poseidon in a landfill is by a boomerang,

To fight 'em to a standstill like they're the Kuomintang

They are calm to lay a bomb and break the wood with a bat,

Prey upon a prayer palm to take the good with the bad,

Bloody them up major if it's mostly policy,

Study their behavior and the sociology,

Steal the tassel from the crones as they blow the light of matches,

Build their castle from the stones that I go to wipe my ass with,

Kiss a kindred ring and bloody rose to guess your fate and first step,

'Tis a different thing to study those you emulate and worship,

Hide the hatch and the wrong bomb as we bloody up the mattress,

Light a match for the long gone as we study up their tactics,

Yearn to sell the art and weapon on a planet with its face gone,

Learn to tell apart the legend from the man that it was based on.

Ash Herds the Elephants

Force the patience still to panic in a lie to doubt the new me,

Corporations kill the planet and we cry about a movie,

It's so rain will fall to cover scents or grade the gold in fucking tents,

It's sustainable in sustenance - afraid to hold the bucket since!

Knapping flints and unavailable to trust the hearts to quiver,

Ashy prints are as indelible as tusks to carve a river,

Rock the camera down where night is on the end's serrated nails,

Propaganda now divides us on unprecedented scales,

The doctor mends the fall like it's fuck staying quiet,

A rock could end it all and we're stuck playing pious,

No one loves 'em like a shit sack as their coffee joins the creamer,

So, it's fuck 'em if they sit back and they wanna point a finger,

To fill a fate as aimless with our essential engine gears,

Facilitate the changes like architectural engineers,

Fill the fist with lonely, free tones as you cook the cross in turmeric,

Build a bridge of only keystones as we look for jobs to burn 'em in,

Grimy sails stall the flames if they smell like shit and spuds,

Time derails all the trains like an elephant in love,

Choose your lies like CeeLo Green and you'll just write a stupid verse,

Utilize an Elohim and unify the universe.

Apu Nahasapeemapetilon

Revolution is in anguish as it's lowered to the deck,

Evolution of a language happens slower than the tech,

Pass by the art of rhyme to first doubt sheisty lessons,

That's why it's hard to find the words now unlike these weapons,

I douse the tears of corpses with a bucket for the bond,

A thousand years of horses and a hundred with the bomb,

We reach up in obscurity when near the setting lock,

We beef up on security in fear of getting shot,

Pits burn a thousand birds after camping through the next step,

Kids learn about the slurs faster than they do the sex ed,

Buy a whore with voice to comment and go back into the grind,

I support the choice to flaunt it, but don't act like it's a rhyme,

Death this evening is as broken as if page two was the end,

Flesh is fleeting in the moment like a 'thank you, cum again!',

Cut and lacerate the saws as the rooms burn the fuel free,

'Cause it's animation flawed when the toons turn to cruelty,

Blood you drink for sips and vat as you set the wood aflame,

What you think, you're Fritz the Cat, and they never could complain?

Read the part I care less than the thoughts I hurl by it,

Keep the art in fair text and then watch the world buy it.

Castration of Language

Guide this thumb or gun to some crime like a pride from sea to school,

I was young and dumb at one time and I tried to be as cool,

Test me like a condiment with payment from a student,

'Edgy' was a compliment and 'gay' meant that it's stupid,

I do repent on this day as the photo runs aground,

The stupid shit that kids say when they know no one's around,

Band-Aids laid in cold snow as we pass the glasses on track,

Man, they've made a whole show that we laugh our asses off at!

How far is it to wade in on your last night of a crux?

South Park is in my state and then I pass by for my drugs,

Man missed a buck up through the bay in a city's dying crimes,

Can't give a fuck what you say when I'm busy writing rhymes,

Eat a brick and chew this fir if you come to die as truth is,

Be a dick and use a slur as you justify its usage,

Stand by truth and rue the blanket as the victim grips his luck,

Man, I used to do the same shit and I didn't give a fuck,

We crush the steel pyramid's rig as Fates divine through Earth,

Because the real lyricists dig the crates to find new words,

Taking ten down a coast sun from its last day to vanquish,

Making men out of most scum doesn't castrate the language.

[Intermission]

ALEX:
So, you understand what we're doing right? No confusion?

STEVEN:
Yeah, yeah, I got this.

ALEX:
Okay then. . . Ladies and gentlemen we are back from our commercial break, and up next is contestant, Steven Arthur! Okay Steve, which topic do you choose?

STEVEN:
It's Steven and I'll take 'Rhyme & Reason' for $1,000, Alex.

ALEX:
Alrighty then and we have 'Rhyme & Reason' for a thousand! The question is: which poet has had the most profound effect on rhyming literature in the last 2,000+ years?

-BUZZ!!!-

STEVEN:
Who was Big Sal.

ALEX:
Was that a question?

STEVEN:
Wha- No. The answer, I answered the question. The one for a thousand.

ALEX:
My goodness you'll have to excuse me – I ate a little too much ass this morning and am really feeling that shit.

STEVEN:
At least you won't get cancelled; I had to fake my death to get here.

30.

Joseph Stalin

A tower crushed the cenotaph as hours rushed to pin it back,

Devour dust of Leningrad and power us — the Men in Black,

Swallow coke and rock to get yer beers in store to pad or check,

Stalin photoshopped his pictures years before we had the tech,

Something evil's now amuck with its energy balls ample,

Cutting people out of books with his enemies all cancelled,

Decry a golden mattress as I pick a view to stay,

Apply his olden tactics to the shit they do today,

Fools drink the air for less if to quake the whole city,

You'll think I'm scared of death 'til I take you all with me,

I need hell to buck or blast if grams are not a good thing,

The sweet smell of succotash that Grandma's always cooking,

To send the heat from pistol to the market of their grains,

A memory is fickle so we carve it in our chains,

Tweak your banjo as we punch it back to play in poor new housing,

People cancelled for their country happened way before 2000,

Plus, my soul's cold as ever like the cobalt and leather,

'Cause we grow old together but we won't mold the weather,

A choice doesn't hoist us to the evil that is rotten,

A voice for the voiceless as the people are forgotten.

So Shady

Go to kick the fence and bully in a glow to stain the dead,

So, significance is sullied when we go to paint it red,

Cats see zappers they'd condemn as they smile at their kill,

As these rappers hate on Em in denial of his skill,

Sights see everybody's fractures leaking loss and not phlegm,

I've seen plenty of these rappers keep him off their Top Ten,

Blow this engine in a practice and a too-filthy vision,

So, opinion is subjective but the truth really isn't,

When we see souls someone found fly to now stay in memoriam,

Many people underground try to downplay the decorum,

Lots occurs placed in back when better men would like to know ya,

Got my first taste of rap from Eminem and Mike Shinoda,

Throw my dinner mints and TV in a show that held us still,

So, I've been here since the EP and I know to relish skill,

Folks feel better now that real men are still dipshit as the rest,

Though I'll never sell a million, I will rip it as the best,

If the dancer's dress won't slay me, then we try to say we smoke,

With the practices so shady that they lie to stay afloat,

Picture mops and a shoe by the soulless in this prison,

Give the props if they're due as I stole this with the rhythm.

Robert Johnson

Finding you to cop a U and punish few off the brew,

I'ma do what Amadou and mamas too often do,

Leach the panic out the fine tip to still preach it to the homes,

Teach the planet how to rhyme it and I'll leave it with my bones,

The mime won't go bite on the fingers if they're not there,

A rhyme so lo-fi that it lingers in the hot air,

Touch the wing by the spring on the path the water launched in,

Pluck a string like a king or the jazz of Robert Johnson,

Tell 'em all I'm a perro once I load the shot I shat,

Sell my soul to the Devil just to go and rob it back,

Ditch the gamut up in panic; final visions drown in pain,

Bitch, you cannot fucking have it – I will piss it down the drain,

Eyes so bruised they cry for help to still flip the stone path,

I will crucify myself and I'll kick my own ass,

'Fore I let you go define me and the shit you wanna see,

War is next to load the timely if it hit upon a tree,

If the wallets now fit the best of thighs to pick these jeans,

As the smallest outlet electrifies the biggest dreams,

Say the food's filled with lie if it cost most our blood,

Play the blues 'til I die at the crossroads for good.

The Caged Bird Dies Twice

Know the old days feel as sound as more independent played,

Yo, if OJ's still around and George Zimmerman is paid,

A step to settle this sick shit as crowds crowd the jail,

They let that little bitch Rittenhouse out on bail,

Once you blink, you're nothing loved on your final days at peace,

'Cause you think you're fucking tough 'til the rifle breaks your teeth,

Passing Windsor in the midst if this is Jenga for a war,

Affluenza for the rich and influenza for the poor,

See through being more alive than the rigs that blast gas

Free Mumia 'fore he dies for the pigs and last laugh,

Canopies to peek the weather if it's built two as divine,

Man, you're free to speak as ever, but to kill you is the crime,

The tips that bend the quill will respect the stone flower,

They lynched Emmett Till to protect their own power,

In the rain that any wash them in to burden what is free,

And the same with Jesse Washington to burn him at the tree,

A word it weighs in zeitgeist as you take it back to play peace,

The bird you cage will die twice if you make it have its babies,

Hand it over at the bridge while we're lighting up the floor,

Cancel culture for the rich while dividing up the poor.

Jesus Christ

We wear no truer beacon than real hats and filthy vice,

Be careful who I speak on if they'll have to kill me twice,

Buy no beer to bomb the breath like the smoking then applies,

I don't fear the song of death if I wrote it when alive,

Time to still pack the chrome for the hit that runs to inns,

I'm the real macaron; you're the shit that comes in tins,

A shallot with a hard cut and a lonely glass of all the tea,

They sell it at a mark-up, but it's only half the quality,

Stripping stables for a horse as they whip up blacker tea,

Tipping tables like they're whores as I give it back for free,

If a potato came to me in the burnt dreams of dead men -

To enable slavery with the 13th Amendment,

Push a brink to hand it over in distinction of the ditch,

'Cause they think that cancel culture is extinction of the rich,

A bomb dropped with big truths on the night that held us out,

A long walk to lick boots, so you might as well just bow!

To import the knives and cupboards as a sea will find its shells,

To support the rights of others is to free the mind of self,

Chickadees that sell them brandy if they send and bear the pinot,

Sip their teas by Calvin Candie and for Quentin Tarantino.

How Many to Bury Wounds?

Now any hours earned for the sake of bad things,

How many flowers burned like the Rape of Nanking?

A tomb weathers half its life for after life it feels,

The wound festers sacrifice for acolytes it heals,

Twirl thoughts inside the soldiers with their choice pride in notions,

Girls taught to hide their shoulders as the boys hide emotions,

Each is someone in their life if you hate 'em on their best day,

Teachers rub 'em on their thighs as they take 'em to the next state,

Dig back these troubles buried at the houses by the stream,

With half these fuckos married and their spouses like a string,

Throw a bitch that fucks boys to no less than much choice,

Go unstitch the plush toys like no kids with crushed joy,

Seize the pen and etcher's pad to decry the dying soldier,

Be the friend you never had and supply a crying shoulder,

Stitch a stoolie to his spy in a sauna filled with shells,

Kids are bullied 'til they die and they wanna kill themselves,

Cut the lights and drown the soldier in a separate filthy candle,

But you cry about a culture that is never really cancelled,

Known to nut up and beat this with a sword and gun to grease,

Grow the fuck up and see this with a heart upon your sleeve.

Richard Ramirez

Seed the grass with dead money in a ditch that's red-green,

Eat that ass like Ted Bundy with a stitch like Ed Gein,

Fatal pride can do a bitch in and depose a few to perish,

They will write to you in prison and propose to you a marriage,

It's my solemn sea surmounting trees that bury whittled bastions,

With psychology surrounding each and every little action,

Through another hand as hopeless, shut the ferry and the seal,

You can understand the motives but to marry is surreal,

Eves that grow through a hot handle pay to bust a dick in there,

Even so you are not cancelled, maybe just a stigma here,

Who took tens of pearls to pay for new grass we're now shearing?

You could end the world today and you'd have a crowd cheering,

Spin the wrist from sun to planet and the dead birds in the rain,

In the gist to understand it and the efforts of the same,

Few can make a sucky hand to still mold you like an army,

You can rape their fucking fam and they'll hold you but a party,

Carried in big, cutting waters at a sea to seek for trees,

There're some sick fucking monsters that are free to speak their piece,

The danger is as nuanced as a blackout for the rebels,

To anger is to humans but to act out is to devils.

An Open Window Speaks of Books

Heavy, bloody rain is on me as you move to pad the crease,

Everybody came for Johnny 'til the truth had spat its teeth,

And a user has a future as it guards this mythic path,

The abuser is accuser in this narcissistic gas,

Though we smoke the club like indo or a deader zombie eye,

So, we open up the window and we let the laundry dry,

Too good to buy a wedding ring's respect if it's a friend's,

You shouldn't strike on anything except in its defense,

Two-inch leg stubs stall and stump it and inspect it in its eyes,

Humans make up all this dumb shit and expect it to survive,

Piss my weight in yellow tone as the best innovation,

It's like playing telephone with the next generation,

As the berries mash no golems on the old vines we found rooting,

The canaries have all fallen and the coal mines are now booming,

Frisk a ninja's sleeve in a fight pose to better get a team,

It's an industry that's unlike those we've never ever seen,

Bodies wet, shot, and last picked for the bash in their graves,

Johnny Depp got his ass kicked and you laughed in his face,

Dread is lit and sees the fuse as the king that's nary killed,

Yet to sit and be accused is a thing that's very real.

Richard Pryor

Fenders turn to fit your tire or the stencils of the cities,

Tempers burn like Richard Pryor in the temples of the titties,

Broken chains host the flames of folks and dames to gross the gains,

Toast to change most arranged for stoves in range of oats and grains,

The spear will spread the sage to the oaks and candy coffin,

Appear upset on stage like the ghost of Andy Kaufman,

Razing desert bombs and dungeons starved by ephors and the peons,

Aging echelons above us arch to eat stars for the eons,

Toast a beer once as icy; lost the ball dunked to cart,

Those revered just as highly often fall just as hard,

Fight the stick-up to the grave with the gun missing some,

Light the strip up in a blaze 'til it's 1:51,

I won't rhyme to sell the money or bury minefields like the birds,

I don't find Chappelle as funny and Jerry Seinfeld is the worst,

The last door is hardly but a ton of other fetty,

I laugh more for Charlie than his younger brother Eddie,

Oxen strip the shores with good pull like the season strips the pole,

Watching civil wars like football as I see this shit unfold,

Reach for deadly spears to push when afraid to riddle these,

Even Gretzky cheered for Bush to invade the Middle East.

Carry a Buck for Me

Golden grills to quit a crack house with the stew in pot and bedlam,

Rolling hills that hit like blackouts when you grew to not expect them,

New tenants are subjected to their new tests and their god,

Eugenics was perfected in the US and abroad,

A cactus and a crayfish when they stand guard as flesh rots,

They practiced on the natives like Anarcha Westcott,

The dirt that holds the chariots will dig us from the stone,

A purpose so nefarious it picked us as its home,

Bury luck on the mission if it seemed to cease in signage,

Carrie Buck was a victim that they deemed as 'feeble-minded',

The defiance rears to kill me with the skin that water douses,

The asylums here were filthy and akin to slaughterhouses,

Ask the murder courts for facts as abrupt as lucky digs,

As the workers force these calves then to suck their fucking dicks,

Miss the map if there's no people on the brink of daily driving,

It's a practice that's so evil that you think I may be lying,

Reaching reapers as they're shifting with their flesh ephemeral,

Teaching creatures of the living that their deaths are preferable,

To thunder by the children as you aim into the node,

You wonder why I'd kill men and then hang them in the road.

Francisco Franco

We sear 'em with a bone bleached to char the oaks and weed,

The fear of the unknown leads to darker roads indeed,

The icy planes of arguments are suitable for markets,

The drive for change is arduous and beautiful regardless,

Despite the winter's wants with the sober sons defecting,

Ignite the spinster's sconce when the soldiers come collecting,

Pass it back to clasp the gadget on a vast and grand atlas,

Half adapt to grasp the magic like the wrath of *Pan's Labyrinth*,

To crash and land action on the last cup that is gold,

I cash the cans back in as I pass up what is sold,

Ban the bat shit and the coal in the cap's detention gown,

And it's tacit if it's told on the aforementioned ground,

Tsk a task with tension in town and a tusk to cull or pass through,

If it has the wrench inbound to then bust a fallen statue,

Seek no dream that meant a mean fuck in the bed or gunman's house,

People seem content to clean up in the stead of someone else,

Ink a pen to press it back in to the ashen shores with God stuck,

We pretend it never happened as the last of doors is locked up,

Hum the part of spells that's missing from the peak and on a pike,

From the heart of hells or prison as they speak into the mic.

A Show Jake Watched in Fake Horns

I stand so tall to others and they fled the night plane,

They cancel all the colors and they let their white hang,

Knees to brace for truth in font while we read to seek facts,

Feed these snakes the foods they want while you feed the sheep scraps,

Teachers pushing deep to function (sleep is nothing!) for the show,

Reapers crushing repercussions steeped in cushions and the glow,

Read my rhyme in your palms on the last day it writhes,

Bleed ya blind as the bombs when the flashbang arrives,

Throw a gun to fuck the system on a sick fiend's quest,

"Oh, my son is but a victim to the big, mean Left!",

Shades of prism grace the vision like the pico due with lime,

Favoritism pays the prison so its people do the time,

To step in place and be low like a C-note for the weed dude,

A better taste to eat though like it's Miklo with the street food,

Through the bough of flame and forest still indeed an imperfection,

To allow this shame before us will concede an insurrection,

Just to build back bridges left by a seed and hundred days,

'Cause they kill Black kids for less while they feed the Trumpist craze,

The government is hard to bury – piss to spill in their laps,

A punishment so arbitrary, systems will collapse!

Josef Mengele

Few won't write it up as secret if they reach the house to tear it up,

You don't like it but you leave it and you flee to South America,

Towards the flowers in our view if they're all placed nigh to relish,

Force the cowards then to do what they always try to tell us,

End the ride in bramble culverts with a white truck lost to jack,

Genocide is cancel culture when they're wiped up off the map,

Terrorizing simple goals to the pyramids and death,

Sterilizing little souls with experiments to test,

A mop to push no blood pan if its village burned endearment,

The doctor was no good man 'til the children learned to fear him,

This is mostly hate and anger in the increments of thoughts amiss,

Disassociate the danger when the dissonance is cognitive,

Bust the bats in respect held as gory as the plot,

'Cause the cracks on a neck tell the story of a god,

From OC to Genesis with a bet that kings drown,

The crow's feet are codices that'll let our wings down,

Stacking dice to cope on fair days; acting nice as smoke or bear mace,

Cracking ice like open airways back to rise like broken stairways,

Eat the brain beneath the ground with a metal spoon of lies,

Lead the train to leave the town as the rebels soon arrive.

The Hill We Die On

At the consummation of a date wasn't lust found for loving,

The pronunciation of a blade doesn't much sound like cutting,

Destinies are then darker than the evil and the fear,

Rest in peace to the martyrs and the people of the year,

Tell us pack a pistol when the legions are against y'all,

Selfless, sacrificial, and the seasons are as special,

It's really cold to build a fence or seal the mesh when home alone,

A hilly knoll to Gilgamesh reveals the flesh so culpable,

I yield to Death and told the fool of this and this to fight the law,

I build a nest so notable the bricks and sticks ignite the straw,

It's a distant light and maw in the book they say is nasty,

With a bishop white and raw when the rook awakens lastly,

The helpless can't go serve the ball if fear is deemed a thing of truth,

A hellish slant so vertical that spirits seem to cling to roofs,

Fight the nearest team of sleuths and their eyes to split the crowds,

Like if lyrics dream of booths and the mics to spit themselves,

Face the power when I rhyme this with these unique guns of mine,

Raise a flower for the finest in a boutique just as fine,

Mesh the siege with the evil and hopes tilled with the okra,

Rest in peace to the people and those killed in Kenosha.

Eldridge Cleaver

See us broken down like Death's toys when his axe is draping linen,

Cleaver wrote about his exploits when he practiced raping women,

Cease to kill the joy of dying on a wretched plate or pan,

People still enjoy his writing as they separate the man,

No one push for extinction once the day adjourns it after,

So, when does the distinction come to play in terms that matter?

To unwind and see an offer as a real hell to push though,

You can write and be a monster and they'll still sell your books bro,

Cruising down the country hills if nothing was actually hill,

Losing out on money deals is something substantially real,

Up the basics when you've said it all and to speak is an assumption,

But to place it as a pedestal is the peak of this dysfunction,

Seek no turnip/bunny crowd once the beans would age with ice,

People worship money now 'cause the means could change their lives,

Unnerving this flying man-mouse are the birds to taste his tale now,

Conservatives crying 'handouts' are the first to take a bailout,

Pumping shit to clean is nasty and the homie knew of pine,

Jumping ship is seen as classy by the only few in line,

Dolls in death will test the buffer as confluence sprawls the gutters,

All the rest are left to suffer and influence all the others.

Underneath a Downtown Rug

Now clown fun like Bugs 'round ground touched in trust,

Downtown under rugs now found wasn't us!

Could we tell 'em each to laugh with a busted ooh-wee?!

Woody Allen bleached his cast and he lusted Soon-Yi,

The banshee arrives softly at the tent to pluck its pick,

Polanski survived Nazis and then went and fucked a kid,

To die over Reagan who has since had you in a ghetto,

You cry over Meghan too if Prince Andrew is a pedo,

Calm supplied the Dutch in the palm to write as such,

Zombified in dust and then bombed inside a bus,

On to plight and pus on the drama side of cups,

Conquer, fight, and push in a longer night than us,

The dumb monkeys shit their pen with ties to Caligula,

The dust bunnies live again and rise like Bunnicula,

It flies as the kestrel comes and hunts tons of geese,

A prize to the pendulum's conundrums at ease,

Come stay 'til we are done and the cars are a blast,

One day we'll see the sun from the stars like a gas,

In principle as lively as the lives we rest in stone,

Invisible as eyes see in the icy metronome.

46.

Hugh Thompson Jr.

Drop a stick in water due at the papers weighed beneath me,

Chop a chip on chopper two as the traitors trade a treaty,

Ruthless clippers shaved a spell as they burnt the skin with salt,

Lucius Rivers made it hell for the servicemen's revolt,

Staying heated at the markets in the towns by that one tree,

They were treated like they're garbage and denounced by the country,

He burnt it in his view and earned his ones from a ten,

He turned to his crew and turned his guns on his men,

Vellum bare as the feet throws opinions up to take,

Held them there with the heat so civilians could escape,

They penalize you often for the wrong bats and the pad,

They demonized Hugh Thompson and the comrades that he had,

They support the core principles of bastards in their way,

They reward the war criminals and hazards of their pay,

Thoughts are in the fire with its evil still applied,

Thompson was pariah with his people vilified,

Test disease on random men with poems leaving woes in vain,

Best believe they cancelled him and no one even knows his name!

Put the blame on me or him when the hurdles fool the rookies,

What a shame to be a man when the world's full of pussies.

Pyrrhic Victory is M.A.D. (Mutually Assured Destruction)

Write a bigger book of violent logs to best use for the dead,

Like I give a fuck if Biden's dogs are rescues or they're bred,

Shock is checking if we live through like a therapist's own shtick,

Stop deflecting every issue when the narrative won't fit,

Bits of lion dung to step in when we burn this mythic field,

Kids are dying up in Yemen and the journalists are killed,

Just supporting of a rhyme on zeniths if fit to climb,

'Cause reporting on a crime is seen as the bigger crime,

Judo kicks to box a window as you pass the ball and smile,

You don't give the cops your info but they have it all on file,

You're buying strictly indo with this pot I'm crumbling nigh,

You try restricting info but you're not a fucking spy,

Your purpose isn't near you if it came through like a check,

Conservatives will cheer you when they hang you by the neck,

Criminals appear too and then move through with the lead,

Liberals will cheer you when they shoot you in the head,

It's the third degree of solemn doubt that's born to god as great,

Gift the currency that's all in clout to form the plot to break,

It's the courtesy of calling out the warning shot we make.

Adolf Hitler

Pose the pulpit by the back and the fair funk or fiddler,

Folks insulted by the fact we compare Trump to Hitler,

Know the injury defeats in this industry displayed,

So, the history repeats with its misery delayed,

I'd have took this war to Man like a fair fight on Baio,

Buy this book before it's banned and beware Mike Pompeo,

Dim the lamp and zeitgeists if it's too late to tell,

In the land of white knights is a crusade they held,

By the three-day post and station like the triptychs in the right hand,

Try to remake most the nation in the image of a white man,

Inspected like a prion glitch; expected to then die a bitch,

Inject it by a dying bridge; inflicted by a lionfish!

Kill the deer at the spring as it gives you to death,

Feel the pierce of the sting as it rips through the flesh,

Dust a hangar on the beach from the tower pool as night goes,

What's the danger of a speech when the crowd is full of psychos?

If the clock will then tick fast, and we fail to come out here -

It's like dropping a lit match on a trail of gunpowder,

End the night with stronger bottles in the back by their own mess,

When they cry for Tom MacDonald to then act like they're oppressed.

Don't Rush the Reaper!

Too tall to handle them fears if war is plain to us,

You called to cancel Em years before we came for Rush,

So sinful in festivities — hop hippity in Hanes,

Your several sensitivities; proclivity to change!

Duck the bigger bridge in town if we ride to hit no switches,

Fucking hypocrites abound and they cry like little bitches,

Look, we're done reporting fracas for the right to place the words,

Fuck your Trump-supporting sagas as we fight to save the Earth,

Stones we push to keep this dirt for a luncheon that is tepid,

Don't you rush the reaper's work when he comes in to collect it,

Share the coffee pots and legend that so softly haunts the sky,

"Everybody wants a heaven and nobody wants to die!"

A colder pine and canopy are crooked as a fallen line,

I stole that line from Apathy and put it in a holorime,

Dead Apollos strip for sex as it picks the beds to stain,

Let the hollows rip your chest as it flicks the flesh to flame,

Coke and goods are sold to rackets on the day to dust 'em nigh,

Open books on broken caskets as they pay for us to die,

Shape these existential devils like they're talcum in a pillow,

Take the presidential medals and then smelt them to a dildo.

Muhammad Ali

Find the words I hope are real when I pacify the pack,

I'm the first to notice skill and the last to cry 'Attack!',

Stick to cantrips if they step in and so staring at their kill,

If the status of a legend has no bearing on its skill,

The desert hills can paint us as the king that meets the ghost you,

We measure skills and greatness as a thing to be opposed to,

Equal cooing for the woes to shed the leering of the damned,

People booing for their foes instead of cheering for their fam,

Who would see this face forever on a real bus that came through?

You could be the greatest ever and they'll still love to hate you,

Best surmise it's my foes with my gloves on their bod,

Death arrives with its crows like the doves of a god,

Quick to quiver at a coal if soliloquies are sold in a venture of the week,

Fish a river of the souls if deliveries or goals are a measure of the meek,

Tuck your crutch in a cramp for the sum of sake and sight,

Put your gloves to the champ and then come and take a ride!

Dead to me and our whole club when the fans are fit to kill,

Let us see if it holds up when they cancel it for real,

Sip on family loss as artists with a cry cast in death,

Into gravitas and darkness if I die as the best.

Everybody's a Villain in Someone's Story

He's still cooking through the pain if the lyrics fight fair,

People looking who to blame when the mirror's right there,

Throw your girl in this air as you slide into her breasts,

No, the world isn't fair, but we fight it to our deaths,

We describe our pains at home when it's mostly vain (still barren),

We inscribe our names in stone with the hopes the rain will spare them,

Why glare into the bottle if my pistol is all I feel?

I stare into this grotto with a fist full of dollar bills,

Still cocking back a gun to feel witless on this course,

I'll fuck up rap for fun and I'll shit this on its corpse,

Time to put me pantomime if I'm stating some are feds,

I'm the Boogeyman of Rhyme and I'm waiting under beds,

Bet your block simply to blow it through a vacant vein to fill it,

Never thought it'd be a poet who would take the game and kill it,

Pinching wenches on their sin sense with their infants' independence,

Inching ninjas into djinn dens and the engines at the entrance,

Pendergrass is at the ball with heavy blasts as rackets fall,

Get it past a tattered hall with sweaty sacks like racquet ball,

Bust a black eye like you're Bane on a binge of hell you hid,

Just the bad guy that you blame for the sins you shall commit.

Elvis Presley

Cut trees spread like briar on a bed of duck/cow shit,

Chuck D set the fire when he said to fuck Elvis,

Plus, it's disassociation asked when no one's gone with peers,

'Cause this misappropriation has been going on for years,

Gassy grills that all leak dead into the ant bits of the slits,

As we steal a colleague's credit like a sandwich from the fridge,

No one waits to numb the day here like the sailors ask civilians,

So, the great succumb to failure and the failures have opinions,

Throw some picture split up the brink in its own decided look,

No one gives a shit what you think 'til you go and write a book,

Selfish pride of a quitter as the dollie pads its brakes,

Elvis died on the shitter and then Ali had his shakes,

Build it back to brag of view or the snow and icy wall,

Silva snapped his leg in two and then oh the mighty fall!

Freefall still faced with forces of the finest friends you'll meet,

We all will place our torches at the highest mental peak,

Diss in rhyme or punch the floor with the wild words of sages,

'Tis a time for love and war like the childbirth of ages,

Show the waistband has weights banned and fake fans the most,

So, we face Man at Graceland and take stands to toast.

An Opinion on a Boycott

Gut the bunny nearer Auschwitz when as bonafide in our book,

Put your money where your mouth is if you don't then buy a product,

Toast a ton of spit or tears to amend the plan too,

Folks have done this shit for years but pretend it's brand new,

It's my following of nuance like the pigeons that a boy caught,

It's psychology of humans and opinions on a boycott,

Hear the dirt building flowers on the corpses new to rains,

We're the first feeling power when it courses through our veins,

Bitch, you suck like agate rock as I pack my bowl clean,

Hit you up like Static Shock when I zap the whole screen,

Standing back on cold cream with the milk and spittle filthy,

And attack an old dream as you feel a little guilty,

Hammers still commit to build thee and it's easier to race,

And if still this shit will kill me then it leads me to the grave,

Ban the queasy from the date and the easy from the dick,

And uneasy as a blade as if Skweezy on a trip,

Write to see me on her clit like it's Fiji in the rain,

Like it's TV for a kid as it keeps me entertained,

Throw away your keys and call and some pointers half in bold,

So, I say to leave it all and come join this #CancelCult.

Charlie Murphy

Need to come up with stone hearts as the gunman shoots the pyres,

Be the sum of your own parts and as someone who inspires,

Shake the pages from the spring and a poem out of hiding,

Take the sages under wing as you show them how to write it,

Write the app code and apply what the track treats us to,

Like an Afro Samurai or like Black Jesus too,

The epiphany, it tires, cut the chase and when we're all in,

Creativity inspires what we place into the cauldron,

A past rose of desire like the next new set of triplets,

Surpass those you inspire as the best who ever did it,

Attention surrounds anything if passions have then died,

Intentions are now everything when actions are applied,

Facing whales in their death as they shape the ground like rocks,

Blazing trails for the rest as they take you down a notch,

Blast through with inhibitions like a fact of your mom's papa,

Statute of limitations like for Afrika Bambaataa,

Bust up a ball and piss blood to watch us crush a round thing,

'Cause what they call a witch hunt is often just accounting,

I'm down to bust a bitch for his columns, crowds, and country,

I count injustices like a comic counts his money.

[Outro]

To change the world, one must understand that people will model themselves but won't listen. . .

We may dance on the hottest of coals, but only through trials and tribulations is the wheat separated from the rye and the oat from the chaff – and at the end of such a day are our feet let free to hang in the icy waters of redemption.

We ache for a world where peaceful transactions and scientific medicine are not held hostage by monstrous and money-hungry capitalists or any others who would take advantage of such a situation.

Believe survivors when they tell you what the monsters did to them, because the chances that they are lying are so low that you just made an ass of yourself assuming that they were.

After all, you would want people to hear you out, right? And to validate your pain and not simply make a mockery of it for the world to stand and laugh at?

We all come from a mother and all return to the dust, so let this be a lesson that no one is above you on this planet we call home.

All art is merely an expression of the self or the self's surroundings, and all pain is masked behind an emotion. Let your strength be the key that unlocks all other facets of your life, and do not fall prey to those that cry like bitches about, 'Cancel Culture'.

Don't be tolerant of the intolerable (the facilitation of fascism or injustice), as turning a blind eye to this makes a man on a global podium yell that he has been cancelled. Money is not the true self.

P.S. Unionize Amazon

www.ingramcontent.com/pod-product-compliance
Lightning Source LLC
Chambersburg PA
CBHW021146020426
42331CB00005B/916